NATURE'S WAY
A SENSE OF BEAUTY

Patrick O'Sullivan lives in Callinafercy, Co. Kerry. Previous publications include *I Heard the Wild Birds Sing*, *A Country Diary*, *Letters to the Earth* and *A Girl and a Dolphin*.

Nature's Way

A SENSE OF BEAUTY

PATRICK O'SULLIVAN

VERITAS

Published 2011 by
Veritas Publications
7–8 Lower Abbey Street
Dublin 1, Ireland
publications@veritas.ie
www.veritas.ie

ISBN 978 1 84730 323 3
Copyright © Patrick O'Sullivan, 2011

10 9 8 7 6 5 4 3 2 1

A catalogue record for this book is available from the British
Library.

Designed by Barbara Croatto, Veritas
Printed in the Republic of Ireland by Gemini International, Dublin

Veritas books are printed on paper made from the wood pulp of
managed forests. For every tree felled, at least one tree is planted,
thereby renewing natural resources.

Though we travel the world over to find the beautiful, we must carry it with us or we find it not.

R.W. EMERSON

Contents

Introduction

*If spring came but once a century instead of once a year,
or burst forth with the sound of an earthquake and not in
silence, what wonder and expectation there would be in all
the hearts to behold the miraculous change.*

H. W. LONGFELLOW

It is clear that the ancient Irish had a sense of beauty. Time after time, Ireland's poets took the beauty of nature as their theme, celebrating not just the seasons but also the trees and the flowers, the animals and the birds that they saw around them. In the poem 'Summer Has Come', the poet describes the nimble deer, leaping with delight, the cuckoo calling in the woods, the twisted hollies hurting the stag, the blackbird singing in the wood. It was no great wonder, the poet said, for the blackbird thought of the wood as his green and living heritage. In another poem of summer, the poet praises the blossoms that covered the earth, the honeybees winging homeward with the harvest of the flowers, the nectar that they loved so much. The corncrake was heard in the meadow, the waterfall making music of its own, even the breeze making whispered conversations among the rushes. The swallows skimmed the blue, the salmon leapt from the river, the wild flag iris a golden shaft that sprang from the green and wonderful earth. The tone of these poems is wonderfully lyrical and celebratory, enriched with the colours, sounds and scents of nature.

Even great heroes were honoured with images of nature. According to the poem 'Lament for the King', Niall of the Nine Hostages had the hue of foxglove in his cheeks. He was described by the poet as a feast without flaw, the crown of the forest in May. The foxglove is one of the most majestic, most beautiful flowers of early summer, emblematic of the promise of summer itself.

The saints were credited with writing nature poetry of their own, among them St Columcille, who celebrated the fruits of the apple trees away in the west, the blackthorns shining with sloes, the oak woods teeming with mast. Nor did the poets forget the romance of the sea: 'Look out over the great ocean, pulsing with life of every kind. It is home to the seals, lively and splendid. The tide is at its highest.' And what of the scribe, the monk writing in the wood. 'I hear the cuckoo sing to me from the tops of the bushes in his grey cloak. Truly may the Lord inspire me as I write here in the cover of the wood.' Caoilte, the legendary hero of the Fianna, describes the beauty of the well of Tráigh Dá Ban for St Patrick. The watercress was plentiful there, but since its verdure had been neglected, no growth had been allowed to its brooklime. There were deer in the woods around it, deer and dappled red-breasted fawns. There was mast on the trees and fish in the mouths of its streams, the sprays of wild arum lily showing beautifully here and there.

There are many different types of beauty: the beauty of nature, the beauty of the human face and form, spiritual, intellectual and moral beauty. The beauty of nature is at once local and universal, particular and cosmic. For though it touches us at an individual level, it binds us with the universe and all that is in it. The American philosopher R. W. Emerson wrote that every natural feature – sea, sky, rainbow and flowers – had something in it which was not private but universal, something which 'speaks of that central benefit which is the soul of Nature and thereby is beautiful'. The soul, the spirit of nature has within it not just the power of beauty but the power of healing too, mending our brokenness and making us one again, not only with ourselves but with the world around us. There is healing in the woods and groves, the little green copse on the verge of spring, when the heron flaps and flutters on top of the stately pine and thinks of nesting again. There is healing in the meadow, when the blue of the tufted vetch is bluer than imagining and the meadowsweet flowers in thickets in the dampest corners of all. There is healing in the hillside when the golden plovers whistle, calling far and away, and the belling of the stag is heard above the flooding stream. There is healing in the sea when the wild waves rush to the shore and the geese are mere silhouettes brushing the face of the moon.

These days, there are times when it seems that we are obsessed with our own genius, mesmerised with our achievements in the fields of technology and science. So mesmerised, in fact, that virtual reality is more acknowledged than reality itself. We are so enthralled that we are blind to the awe-inspiring wonders of the world around us. I love to stand in the morning and watch the winter sun rise yellow and golden above the darkened ridge of Dromin Hill in Co. Kerry. There is something almost mythical about the sunrise; something mysterious and ancient, harking back to the time of ancient stones and spirals and perfect alignments. It has a kind of splendour that goes beyond syntax and grammar, the dazzling gold of the light washing over the dark ridge of the hill, then spreading upwards and outwards across the sky. It is as though it has been drawn up from some pre-historic well, some ancient pool of brightness by the power of a secret charm inaudible to the human ear. The bare dark boughs of the apple trees are soon stirred by the singing of the thrush; it is as if he too is glad of the sun and the light and the morning. In *King Lear*, Shakespeare speaks of 'the sacred radiance of the sun', but alas it seems as if we have lost touch with the sacredness of sunrise as we have lost touch with so much else that is sacred and beautiful in nature. The poet John Donne, in his Sermons for Easter Day, 25 March 1627, made a very pertinent point about the wonders of nature and creation:

> There is nothing that God hath established in a constant course of nature, and which therefore is done every day, but would seem a Miracle, and exercise our admiration, if it were done but once.

R. W. Emerson picked up on the same theme in his essay on nature:

> If the stars should appear one night in a thousand years, how would men believe and adore; and preserve for many generations the remembrance of the city of God which has been shown! But every night come out these envoys of beauty, and light the universe with their admonishing smile.

There may be much in nature that is fitful and changeful and unpredictable, but there is much that is ordered and beautiful too. Even change has a beauty of its own, in the ever-changing sweep of light and shadow over lonely hills and glens in the warmth of the summer's day. The puffin on the wild seacoast is an envoy of beauty. Likewise the handsome chough when he soars above the sea-green waves and gives voice to his ringing calls. The purple flowers of the knapweed, the nodding blues of the harebell, the yellows and oranges of the bog asphodel; the vigorous song of the wren; the seal on the lonely shore; the red squirrel safe in the arms of the pine; kingfisher, starling and cuckoo – all envoys of beauty.

The beauty of nature gives us all reasons to be glad, reasons to be cheerful every hour of the day, every week of the year. The beauty that we see around us has its own honesty, its own integrity that goes far beyond the shallow and the superficial; when we begin to appreciate it we see something of that honesty and integrity. We see something of that generosity of spirit that informs the whole of creation, from the far seas teeming with fish to the wild woods heavy with fruits, from the meadows crowded with flowers to the long streams running like silver in the wild and lonely glens. Nature has many secrets, and though she may never disclose them all she will always be a friend to those who love her, to those who see beauty in a star, or in the winking of rainy beads when the fern uncurls in the springtime. Nature's beauty is not uniform; rather is it rich and diverse. It can make such a wonderful difference to our lives. Celebrating nature is part of our history and our heritage. It is, in a way, part of what we are.

A Sense of Beauty

In wilderness I sense the miracle of life and behind it our
scientific accomplishments fade to trivia.

CHARLES LINDBERGH

Callinafercy National School, Co. Kerry, was one of those
old-fashioned country schools with yellow-washed walls and a
gabled porch facing the road. It was set in a weave, a wonderful
weave of woods and groves and fields and lanes. Padraig Pearse,
one of the leaders of the 1916 Rising, was a hero of mine.
Though I could not articulate it then, I think I liked him for
his vision, his idealism, his sense of beauty. I knew that he was
a poet, and the only poem of his I knew then, 'The Wayfarer',
struck a chord with me at once. I remember learning it at
school, filled as it was with lovely images of nature: squirrels,
ladybirds, rabbits at evening time. The opening lines took me
by surprise though. 'The beauty of the world hath made me
sad. This beauty that will pass.' I thought that beautiful things
were supposed to make you happy. I liked nothing better than
peering into hedges for birds' nests and eggs in the springtime,
or running in long grasses mid-summer. I loved watching the

goldfinches among the thistle tops in the autumn, hearing the wild swans rise from the river in the still of a winter's day. I don't know if I thought of it then, but at an unconscious level at least, joy and beauty felt one and the same: the twin halves of the same sphere. That was why it was so strange to me that beauty could make anyone sad. Of course, it was not the beauty itself that made the poet sad but the thought of its transience, of it passing away. Even in the very moment of perfection, of achievement, the thought of that transience could not be kept at bay. It was no great wonder then that R. W. Emerson prayed that he might never lose an opportunity to see things of beauty in the world around him. It was as if he too recognised its preciousness, its worth, its transience. That which does not last is all the more beautiful still.

The great thing about beauty is that it is right on our doorstep. We do not have to travel hundreds of miles to see it. Unlike rare and precious man-made things, it is accessible to everyone. We only have to look out our windows and there it is before us. When I sit at my kitchen table, my window frames the daffodils in spring. I love the daffodils, their yellow cavalcade a metaphor for the promise of the season. The roses and the lilies paint a portrait of the summer, the bright-berried shrubs a picture of the autumn. In the winter, my window frames the grove, the fir trees on the edge all gleaming and grey with frost. Even there, at my kitchen table, I have images of beauty before me: the beauty of the seasons. Confucius wrote: 'Everything has beauty, but not everyone sees it.' That is the trouble with beauty. It seems so familiar, so commonplace, at times we hardly give it a second glance, let alone a second thought. Perhaps, like Emerson, we too should pray that we may never lose an opportunity to see it. What could be nicer than a country stroll at any time of the year; perhaps in summer when the yellow flags crowd the margins of the stream, or huddle in damp corners of the meadow, their yellows more vibrant, more beautiful than any mixed by the artist at his work. Or maybe in the autumn, when the pheasant rockets skywards, an explosion of copper and crowing among the clouds of falling leaves. Or perhaps in the winter when the sun finds the snow on the highest mountain peaks and paints them with the crimson of its early morning rays. Or in the spring when the snowdrop peeps from the cold and frozen soil and the tiny wren looks for places to build its nest in the greening all around.

If the beauty of nature made Padraig Pearse reflect on its passing, then the same beauty made W. B. Yeats reflect on his own ageing. When he went back to see the swans at Coole Park after nineteen years, it seemed to him that they had not changed at all. Swans were the ultimate symbol of beauty and immortality in Irish myth and legend. They played a part in many of the well-loved stories, the most famous of all being 'The Children of Lir', so it is no great wonder that the poet thought of them as ageless, changeless and eternal. Their hearts had not grown old, he wrote. It was as though so much had changed in his life in the intervening period, a reflection prompted by his disappointment in love. The swans, on the other hand, did not seem to have changed at all. They were as beautiful as they ever were. It may have been just an illusion, but it is a reminder that if the beauty of nature is transient, then it is also resilient, passed down from generation to generation, seemingly endless. Think of the trees for instance. They bring a kind of permanence to the landscape where they have sometimes stood for hundreds if not thousands of years. In their way, they embody the beauty of nature's architecture. Why should we think of beauty at all? Why should we think it is of any value to us? After all, it can hardly be measured in euros and cents. Keats wrote:

> A thing of beauty is a joy forever:
> Its loveliness increases; it will never
> Pass into nothingness; but still will keep
> a bower quiet for us, and a sleep
> full of sweet dreams, and health, and quiet breathing.

Beauty offers us not only joy but peace, quiet and serenity too. The wood welcomes us with its quiet bowers on long summer days. At this time the pathways are green and winding with mosses and the scent of the honeysuckle hangs heavily in the air. The river's edge sees the otter slip into quiet waters at evening time, unperturbed by the chill of winter's breath, the ripples blue and golden in his wake.

The beauty perceived through the senses is food for the spirit. It is the sustenance, the nourishment that makes the spirit strong. Dostoyevsky wrote in this regard:

… love all God's creation, both the whole and every grain of sand. Love every leaf, every ray of light. Love the animals. Love the plants. Love each separate thing. If you love each thing you will perceive the mystery of God in all, and when you perceive this you will therefore grow to a fuller understanding of it; until you come at last to love the whole world with a love that is all-embracing and universal.

We need beauty more than ever in our lives today as we are relentlessly bombarded with all kinds of images by an omnipresent media, images that are often troubling, disturbing and distracting. We like to think that we are much more sophisticated than those who have gone before us. We like to think that we know more than they ever did, but maybe it is time for us to learn to love again, rediscovering the beauty that is all around us and giving it a place at the centre of our lives. In this way we may rediscover the beauty of simplicity too, the beauty of the simple life lived in harmony with nature, and we may take comfort from it. Only when we value the beauty of nature, only when we learn to love it, do we begin to appreciate that we are part of it too: part of the fabric of the universe that stretches from the stars to the spider's web, from the glittering wastes of ice and snow to the tiny ladybird sheltering from the rain in the thimble of the foxglove.

We are part of the universal spirit that lives and breathes in every living thing, and if our appreciation of the beauty that surrounds us brings us to an understanding of this, then it will surely be time well spent. Being with beauty strengthens our ties with creation, not just with the things we see but with those we hear, feel, taste and touch. What could be more inspiring than the singing of the birds on a fine spring day, their voices blending together in celebration of the season? What is lovelier than the touch of the silken green of the leaves at the edge of summer, when it seems that nature saves its finest for the season of the sun? What is nicer than the taste of blackberries, wild and dark and juicy, or the green scent of the woods when the sun rises yellow and golden behind the dark of the winter hills?

Love permeates beauty: love and belonging. There are times when we can feel alienated from the world around us, alienated and upset by all that we read and hear in the news. This is why it is all the more important to remember that nature is beauty's home, and when we are at one with nature we are truly home. Even the simplest of things – stopping to look at bluebells that stretch far and away under the trees, or gathering windfalls in dewy grasses, hearing the curlew on the lonely shore, or catching the scent of the orchid in the bogs – even the simplest of things can make us feel at ease with our surroundings. Or as the old woman put it, they can make us feel at home in the world again. It is our senses which allow us to perceive the richness and diversity that make up the beauty of the world. Perceiving is only the beginning, for after that comes understanding, appreciation and love. We do not have to know the names of everything in nature to appreciate their value. The butterflies know nothing of the names of the flowers from whose nectar wells they drink. Perhaps we should take our lead from the butterflies by occasionally enjoying nature in this unconscious, unreflective way. Beauty, after all, is the gift that teaches the soul to sing.

Hearing

Never does nature say one thing and wisdom another.

JUVENAL

There is nothing lovelier than standing by the wayside on a
moonlit night and listening to the cries of the lapwings. Their
haunting 'peewit' calls are the essence of winter. The lapwing is
known in Irish as *an Pilibin*, a name that has a lyrical ring to it
and that is wonderfully evocative of the birds themselves. The
calls of the lapwings were very much part of my youth, part of
the magic of childhood winters. Perhaps that is why I associate
them still with all the wonder and romance of the season
itself: moonlight and starlight and the glitter of frosted fields.
E. M. Nicholson, one of the greatest ornithologists of his day,
noted that the cries of the lapwings had a haunting romantic
quality. I do not know if I thought of it then, but every time
I hear their wild delighted calls now I think of them as beauty
given voice, and I am so glad that I can hear them still. The
calls in themselves are not only primal and elemental, they
are evocative of all that is wild and wonderful, of all the tidal
channels and estuaries that glisten and gleam in the moonlight,

of the gatherings of reeds turned ashy and brown in the winter time, of the frosted fields that gather the moonlight to them and make them even lovelier. There is also the plaintive calling of the curlew, the familiar *cur-loo* often rising in pitch at the end. E. A. Armstrong wrote of the wild, beautiful sadness he heard throbbing in the curlew's cry, and there is no denying that the rich whistling does indeed have a hint of sadness in it. However, it still brings the winter's day to life and becomes part of the tapestry of sound along the estuary. Every time I hear the wild bugles of the whooper swans, I think of them bringing the music of the far north to our shores. The sound is wonderfully evocative of all the gleaming wastes of ice and snow that the whoopers have left behind them. The bugling is deliciously wild and free, embodying the freedom of the skies that seems to open out before them. It is as if these beautiful snow-white birds are talking to one another as they go by overhead. Winter would not be complete without the characteristically rolling *rronk* of the wild brent geese in flight. This too contains something of the romance of long journeys, the travelling all the way from eastern Greenland and Spitsbergen. It is as if they, like the swans, bring us the sounds of other worlds, of other places so different to our own. Their calls give us a sense of beauty. And the *wo-wo* barking of the fox in the wintertime, echoing from some silver orchard or field under the light of the moon – it too is like the signature of the season, redolent of the woods and groves and secret trails known only to the fox himself.

Winter gives way to spring, when the blackbird thinks of singing again. How wonderful it is to be able to stand and listen to the blackbird on long spring evenings, the wild and fluted notes filling the place with delight. Listening to this sound is an age-old pleasure, speaking to the spirit still. It has been said of the blackbird's song that it has a mellowness and contentment above all others. This certainly feels true, for the song seems like a celebration of all that is good and beautiful in springtime – greening hedges and fields, flowers and ferns and nests and eggs. The more one listens to the song, the more it becomes an anthem to creation. One of the great things about the blackbird is that he is not always content to stick with tradition. He is quite adept at trying out new compositions, new variations of his own, singing some of the fluted phrases with a quirkiness and individuality that sets them apart from the rest. The song has a fluency too, simple and mellow, but with an unmistakable richness and throatiness. There is no finer expression of beauty, no finer experience than to hear the blackbird sing in the hedge at dusk. It is as if the world has grown still and quiet, spellbound by the beauty of the blackbird's song.

The thrush's song is loud and melodious, incorporating a sequence of repeated phrases. I remember three great cypress trees that grew in the back yard when I was young, visible at a distance on the hill. One of them was our swinging tree, the swing itself no more than a rope thrown over a sturdy branch, a small piece of board serving as the base. It was the best thing in the world to be swinging back and forth in the evening time, the thrush at his song somewhere high among the branches. Sometimes I looked up to try and pick him out there, but most of the time I did not look up at all. It was enough just to know that he was there, just to hear him at his song. It was as if the song and everything about it were part of the rhythm, the pulse of nature in the heady days of spring: the clarity of the notes giving it a charm all of its own. Spring would not be spring without the singing of blackbird and thrush.

At this time the rhythmic bubbling sound of the little egrets can be heard among the firs and pines in the grove. This is the breeding season, and the chorus of bubbling is part of the music on a fine spring day. Their neighbours, the grey herons, are noisy too, their raucous squawking unlikely to be mistaken for the call of any other bird. They indulge in a great deal of flapping and fluttering on the tops of the tallest pines, somewhere at the roof of the sky, and yet the wood would not be the same without them in springtime.

Meanwhile out in the fields, the mare whinnies with delight at the sight of her newborn foal, and the donkey brays with sudden and unexpected gusto. The lambs bleat in answer to their mothers' calls. Rain pitter-patters gently on the silken green of beech and birch. I was once caught in a downpour and was forced to shelter under a great old beech tree for a long time. I heard the melodies of rain that I heard so often as a child. It was as if they were the creation of sky and season, the coming together of both to produce harmonies all of their own.

If there is any sound in tune with the heartbeat of earth, then it must surely be the pouring rain, the silvery drops plopping and splashing on every little silken leaf.

Summer brings the joys of the dawn chorus, one of the most magical sounds on earth, the songs in tandem with the coming of the light. First the robins begin, then as the darkness starts to flicker and fade, the blackbirds and thrushes join in. After that come the great tits and the blue tits, the chiffchaffs, the blackcaps and the garden warblers. Also heard in that chorus is the loud and vigorous song of the wren, the chaffinch and the wood warblers waiting until sunrise to lend their voices to the chorus. Listening to the dawn chorus in a wood in early summer is a full, true, wonderful experience of the beauty that is all around us in nature.

The musical twitter of swallows bringing the sun and the summer on their backs, the soft and muffled calls of the cuckoo in some green and distant grove, the rasping of the corncrake, are all evocative of my childhood summers of long ago. The sound of summer streams, water bubbling gently, softly over stones, is made all the more magical if heard in the quiet secluded splendour of some lonely valley or glen. Like the singing of the birds, it is more than just beauty – it is healing. It is balm for spirit and soul. It gives us the freedom to sit a while and do nothing, to know that the slow life can have its moments too, to appreciate again that sense of belonging that occurs when we are at one with nature. The music of the stream is older than time, yet newer than a summer's day. Lark and linnet are heard in the bogs, the lark pouring out melodies in the blue cascades of sky overhead, the little linnet lost in the rolling gold of furze. The blackcap meanwhile sings from the cover of foliage, his rich melodious song one of the finest of the season; it is no great wonder that he has come to be known as the northern nightingale. The soft summer breeze makes dancers of the leaves, ruffling their silken skirts. The honeybees hum in the wild flowers in the meadow.

Autumn comes and the wind sounds in the woods, stirring the trees and the leaves. The rivulets become swollen with rain. The musical whistle of the golden plover is heard in high places; the belling of the stags flooding the hills and the glens with sound. The fieldfares make their familiar *chack chack* in flight, crowding the hedges and copses in search of the harvest of berries. The redwings make the thinnest of *tseeps* as they fly overhead at night as part of their autumn migration, the sound suggesting something of the fragility, the vulnerability of the birds themselves. The ripened fruit falls, softly thudding on the grasses. The starlings keep up their mimicry as though they always find reasons to be cheerful. The jay gives a scolding scream. Winter comes again, the hush of snow so real, so palpable one can almost hear it. There is no other stillness, no other silence like it in the world. It is winter's breath soothing the world and putting it under its spell. The sense of beauty, the sound of beauty, comes to us in a thousand different ways. It enriches the spirit and soul with the wonderful voices of nature, reminding us again of the richness and diversity that is all around us.

Seeing

People from a planet without flowers would think we must be mad with joy the whole time to have such things about us.

IRIS MURDOCH

Frost flowers on the windowpane, trees and fields; lanes and hedges are silvered, the temperature drops to minus eleven, even part of the river is frozen. A study in beauty – the ice marbled with silver and glitter and frost and light, the sun golden but ineffectual on the far horizon. The whiteness of the mute swans on the far shore looking increasingly radiant. It is as if they are made of the fallen snow. They take to the wing with a great flapping and fluttering, their flight elegant, graceful, almost surreal above the frozen river. It is as if they are creatures of myth and legend come to life, the living breath of the Children of Lir, Fionnuala and her brothers and their companions too. Their elegance in flight is beyond the limitations of language. It is beauty in motion, beauty on the wing, their whiteness outspread above the gelid stillness of the stream. The mute swans are beautiful at any time of year but they come into their own in the winter, their brilliance the perfect complement to the shimmer of snow and ice. It was on a much milder day that I spotted the kingfisher along the estuary. He was orange, chestnut and white, but most of all he was blue: a bolt of electric blue shot from some secret hiding place. There are times in autumn when the kingfisher, if he is still, blends in perfectly with the backdrop of autumn leaves, but he is unmistakable on a misty winter's day. No wonder an old bird book describes his flight as 'resembling a bright blue arrow in its speed and colour'.

The estuary is home to mallards and shelduck too, the latter beautifully coloured, showing a dark-green head and red bill, and richly contrasting black and white and chestnut body. They fly beautifully with slow, shallow wing beats, the black wing tips, white forewings and green speculum readily seen. They bring colour and movement and wonder to the winter scene, the rolling grey of the clouds the perfect backdrop for the splendour of their plumage. The heron fishes in the long-legged pools. A patient fisherman, he has all the time in the world. He is as slow as the lazy river around him.

The heron and his relative, the little egret, have the same flight pattern with head tucked back, long legs trailing behind. The brilliant white of the little egret rivals that of the swan, echoing the snow on the distant hills.

Snowy mountains are mirrored in the water so that it is hard to know what is real and what is not. I share something with the poet Robert Frost. Just like him I had the pleasure of stopping by woods on a snowy evening. I too watched them fill up with snow on the darkest evening of the year, 21 December. It was the heaviest fall of snow in years and it was magical to see the thickening flurries drift down and down again. The fieldfares and the redwings had stripped the scarlet from the green of holly, but suddenly the snow was transforming the hollies into something stranger, more magical still. The snow enhanced the symmetry, the perfection of fir and spruce and pine, so that there was a very real sense of walking in a picture-perfect Christmas card. Lines of fir flanking a snowy aisle in a secret place all of my own. It was as if winter was putting on its finest show and I was so blessed to be a part of it, the snowfall redolent of a childhood Christmas of forty years or more before. I remembered sinking into the snow back then, the whiteness so deep it was as if there were layers of it underfoot. Suddenly I was sinking again, sinking into memory and delight, into the innocent white of childhood. Every dip and hollow was settled and smoothed by the transforming power of the snow; it seemed as if an enchanter had found his way into the woods, veiling the greens with his marvellous whites. A few days later I spotted the handsome red fox crossing the snowy fields and again it was as if beauty were reminding me of its presence.

What would springtime be without the waking of the colours, the stirring of yellows, golds, purples and whites, every one of them springing from their winter sleep with sudden verve and beauty? There is the crocus, the snowdrop and the daffodil, the latter's trumpets as yellow as the morning sun when it glints on the golden windows of the east. The daffodils are a celebration of all that is beautiful and wonderful in spring. They are a reaffirmation too, a statement of faith in the goodness of the season itself: emblematic of an age-old beauty that speaks of rebirth and renewal. The daffodils never grow tired, they never grow weary. They are the untiring spirit of nature dressed in its finest for spring. Once I was cycling in a little country lane, the hedges greening and leafing again, when I spotted a great sweep of bluebells in a little copse nearby. I could not resist the impulse to go and look at them more closely and so, in an instant, I was putting my bike aside and heading across the field. It is beautiful in the springtime to see all those nodding inky blues spreading far and away under the beech trees. I was spellbound where I stood. It was almost as if the bluebells had taken the midnight blues of sky and ocean, distilling them together in some secret process of their own, until at last they had achieved that perfect mesmerising blue. I had to do a bit of searching to find the little shy violets clustered here and there, heart-shaped leaves the perfect complement for the soft blue-violet of the flowers. It would be another day and another place before I would find the wood sorrel, the little green leaflets sleeping in the rain, folded as they were down the central leaf stalk, the white of the flowers showing violet veins. Birds nesting: among them the dunnock or hedge sparrow, eggs the purest of blues. Robin and nestlings crammed into an old iron kettle under the privet hedge, breast like a flame when she leaps onto the rim as if to survey the scene around her.

Rooks busy too, the bluish sheen of their plumage catching the light as though eager to play games with it. The grey wagtail looks more yellow than grey, bowing and bobbing its tail on the dark stone in the stream. The stonechat finds a place in the furze. The jackdaw and his mate happy again in the warm, companionable sun.

The ruins of an ancient abbey lie smouldering in the peace of a crimson sunset. On one of the side walls the magnificent yellows of verbascum, Aaron's rod. The sense of peace and serenity palpable here, the crowded spikes of yellow soaking up the light in the late-evening calm. Only the swallows sweep overhead. Rock rose in the hedge. The last of the columbines, purple and blue. The meadow a haven of flowers, tufted vetch and vetchling and golden trefoil too, the wild blue of the vetch like the blue of summer itself. Foxgloves on parade on a grassy bank, their purple thimbles havens for honey and bumblebees and lovely little ladybirds. Orange montbretia by the wayside still showing the splendour of nature's magic garden, meadowsweet and loosestrife gathering the sun.

Butterflies are like fairies on wings of painted silk. So evocative of summer, a cloud of butterflies in some old forgotten meadow, the magic of painted ladies that come to us on long journeys from the far-flung steppes, the larvae feeding on thistles. An inhabitant of tropical and sub-tropical climates, it cannot survive the winter of northern Europe. When food becomes scarce in its own territories, largely due to drought, it begins to migrate, its power of flight incredible. I remember them teeming in an old meadow by the coast, their upper wings marbled pinkish buff, black and white, the under wing showing the same pattern as the upper. The butterflies were visiting the flowers for nectar, crowding the trumpet-shaped flowers of the mallows too, the latter most likely escapees from the cottage gardens nearby, fringing the line of the strand. What could have been more beautiful than crowds of butterflies in a summer meadow, the fantastic light sweeping the blue of the sky overhead? The sea waves dazzling with light, parallels seeking the shore. The world is changeful, full of imperfection; all the more reason to celebrate perfection when we find it, if only for a moment. Just like the geese in winter, the butterflies come on long journeys. They bring us the romance of far-off places. I remember an old woman and her beautiful butterfly brooch. 'I keep it for the summer,' she said, 'the summer I keep in my heart.'

The fish flash in the water, 'rose moles all in a stipple' as Gerard Manley Hopkins has it. The salmon creates a silver rainbow when he leaps into the air, painting pictures of the majesty of summer. The fruits ripen on the old apple boughs, the skins of the bramleys red and green with dew in the morning. The swallows gather, getting ready for the off. The snipe zigzags in the marsh. The woodcock, marbled chestnut, black and white, finding camouflage among the falling leaves. Yellow, gold and brown, tawny, flame and russet red: autumn's palette at its most beautiful. It is as if the huge old trees are putting on one last show in honour of the season that is in it.

They become studies in unselfconscious beauty, for this is their inheritance, their birthright: the splendour of autumn merely the fulfilment of the promise of spring and summer. There is no mistaking the peace of the colours in the wood of an autumn evening, an antidote to all that is noisy, troubling and distracting in the world around us. Hedgehog lost in dreams, the red squirrel among the pines, likewise the lovely siskin. The stag on the golden hill, the barn owl calls to the night. Winter and spring, summer and autumn, we have hundreds of thousands of ways of seeing the beauty of nature, and in that seeing we nurture spirit and soul. Through the senses we perceive, through the spirit we learn to love a beautiful world.

Touching

The sun does not shine for a few trees and flowers, but for the wide world's joy.

HENRY WARD BEECHER

Nature is a feast for the senses, not least of which the sense of touch. The world is full of textures, even in winter. The smooth grey bark of the beech evokes something of the beauty, the splendour of the tree itself. The oldest of the beech trees stands opposite the ruins of the old Callinafercy schoolhouse. It is the tree of memory and innocence, the touch of it like something lost but still remembered. It brings back echoes of long-lost childhood days, the old tree burgeoning again at the verge of summer, the birds at their song in every part. Now the tree is bare in winter, the husks remnants of the autumn, spiny to the touch. The trunk of the oak grey and full of crevices – signals of its age. They are like badges of honour, vivid reminders of its endurance; it has seen so many seasons come and go and yet it still stands tall in the wood. The elegant lines of the birch, its white bark peeling like paper, the touch of it hinting at secrets in the wordless books of nature. The long bare trunk of the Scot's pine, flaking in scales. Many of the trees here are lapped in mosses, the latter oozy and damp, for the rain is a frequent visitor. The touch of the moss is delicious, for it not only hugs the trees, it makes a carpet for the green and winding ways. Its very softness and luxuriance hints at enchantment, the mosses, the ivies and the wild green arbours of the trees creating a perfect calm.

The sense of peace here is truly wonderful. Wordsworth wrote: 'Move along these shades in gentleness of heart; with gentle hand touch – for there is a spirit in the woods.' The sheep hold forth on the high hills in winter, their very presence softening the lines, the hard angularity of the hills; their soft fleeces contrasting with the cold, hard grey of the unyielding rocks. Stones and crags silently keep watch since the first ages of the world. I rub my hand over the surface of one and I feel something of that stillness, that silence. It is the cumulative stillness of years, the slowness of time perceived in the touch of the stone. I feel the lichens, the crusty patches of ochre and grey that are testimony to the passage of time. I have never stroked the fur of a fox, but as a child I dreamt of doing so. Even now I think of it, and I begin to think that I am still a child at heart. Sometimes I reason that it is only children who appreciate the feathered chill of the snow, the chill that delights them when they feel its softness between their fingers. I still remember the joy of making a snowman. Just as the flowers were the gift of summer so the snow was the gift of winter. 'They're plucking the geese in heaven,' was what the old people said when the downy flakes came down and down again. However, an old woman told me it wasn't that at all, it was 'the angels having pillow fights'. The touch of the snow was the touch of winter, redolent of the icy wastes of the far north and sure to send tingles in every part.

In Irish tradition, St Brigid dipped her toe in the stream on her feast day, 1 February, and all at once the cold left the water. Brigid was very fond of the animals, so she was keen that the cold would retreat before the coming of spring. She travelled around the country on the eve of her feast day, the people not only making crosses of rushes in her honour but sometimes strewing the threshold with fresh rushes too. The softness and freshness of the rushes were a token of the esteem in which she was held. It is a lovely image: the barefooted saint feeling the softness of the rushes underfoot when she came to visit the house. Springtime also brings the lushness of the grasses back to the fields, the donkey rolling with delight in the greenness all around him. Meanwhile, the little hare moulds and shapes the new grasses for her nest as she prepares to give birth to her young. She makes her form by turning around and around in the long grass, then nestling down, pushing her long hind legs behind her, spreading herself out. In this way the grass takes on her impression, the spot where she lays warm to the touch on chilly spring evenings. Touching the flat grass is like touching the breath of the wild, catching it and holding it in one's hand. I remember the tiny leverets in the small hayfield by the house when I was young. I would have given anything to stroke them but I had enough sense even then to know that such things could not be. I remember the bullfinch in her nest, imagining as I did the softness of her downy breast as she nestled on her eggs; her mate keeping cover in the blackthorn thicket nearby. I don't know if I thought of it then, but in the softness and the warmth of that nest, new life was stirring again, life that would one day be heard calling in the orchard's green peace.

I feel the downy leaves of the foxgloves, the thimbles opening upwards along the stem. Wisps of bog cotton, soft as any wool. The neatest of sods, oozy and damp when cut with the slean, patiently drying in the long summer sun. I feel the fleshy rhizomes of the wild flag iris, the yellow flowers erect among the sword-shaped leaves, the dark rich velvety-brown of the reed mace among the meadowsweet and loosestrife.

When I was young, I loved to run in the meadows at the height of summer, the silken swish of grasses like the touch of summer itself. Back then the meadows were teeming with flowers, but it was the touch of the grasses themselves that made it more wonderful. It was lovely just to lie down in them on a lazy summer's day, the azure blue of the sky brushed in broad stokes overhead, the heartbeat of earth heard and sensed among the grasses and the flowers. Then, when the meadows were cut at last, I loved to go exploring in the margins, and when I found a frog, I took it and stroked it, savouring the sleek, chilly smoothness of its skin. Though I did not know it then, there was, in that touch, secrecies of nature that words could not describe.

Along the seashore the prickly sea holly can be found, the pale bluish-green of the leaves with spiny teeth. The warmth of the sand underfoot, again bringing back echoes of carefree childhood days, when running barefoot in the meadow or on the strand seemed like the most natural thing in the world. The ridged splendour of limpets crowded on rocks, the oozy damp of seaweed dripping with brine, the pebbly delights of lonely little rock pools. The brine itself cool, refreshing and light as though it were oozing with the light of the sun – the latter hung like a great golden disk in the sky, radiating warmth in every part. The gulls on the rocks shuffling their feathers as though they can feel it on their backs. The soft wind from the south caresses the shore, skimming over the dunes where the larks were singing in spring. I ran after butterflies and moths and tried to catch them when I was a child, and I feel like doing so again. It hardly matters that I have very little hope of catching one. All that matters is that it is summer and in the moment I am young again. I run after cinnabars and burnets, and at last I catch hold of a burnet. Imagine my delight. It flits and flutters in the dark recess of my hands and I feel the silken touch of its wings against my skin. I cradle it only for a moment, and when I set it free it takes to the air with delight, tossing itself into the sun. The dolphin humps in the green and blue of the sea, revelling in every swell and surge of the brine around him.

Autumn brings the golden fields of grain, the bearded stalks heavy and ripe and laden with goodness. The touch of the grain is the touch of the season itself, the fruitfulness of the hour.

Goldfinches haunt the downy thistle patch, the soft down of the thistles rich in seeds. The apples that hang on the bough are smooth and firm to the touch, for they have gathered up the goodness of summer and keep it within them. They have captured the sun and the light, the warmth of heat-drenched days. There is the softness of autumn mists, of autumn rains embracing the fruits on the trees and making them wink. The blackbird is glad of the shiny pools when the rain comes down in torrents; he revels in the moment, the water soaking every part of him so that when he gives a vigorous shake of his feathers, the shiny drops swim in the air and glitter in the sun. Blackbird bathing in a rainy pool: an easily imagined scene. There is a kind of peace here, a peace and serenity that goes far beyond the shallow allure of our glitzy consumer world.

In my garden, I take my garden fork and begin digging in the earth. It feels crumbly and soft when I take some in my hands. 'It's as fine and as dry as sand,' someone says admiringly of the soil. I take my sapling apple tree and place it in the earth, gathering the soil around it and making it firm. The beady-eyed robin perches himself on the handle of the fork when I am not using it. The young boughs, even the stem itself, is smooth and bare to the touch, but I look forward to the day when the little tree grows tall and strong and the boughs will be clothed with blossoms. In the meantime I wish it the blessings of the sun and the rain, misty mornings and dewy evenings when every part of it will be wrapped in the peace of nature. After the blossoms will come the fruits, shiny and smooth, the touch of them telling of green boughs and mosses and birds at their song. When I feel the good earth between my fingers again, it is as if I am part of the wonderful weave that is nature, as if I too have played some little part in nurturing its promise.

Tasting

Good heavens, of what uncostly material is our earthly happiness composed ... if only we knew it. What incomes have we not had from a flower, and how unfailing are the dividends of the seasons.

JAMES RUSSELL LOWELL

I remember reading an article in which someone described the pleasure of a winter walk in the wood. The day was fresh and bracing, the air itself was tasting as sweet as champagne. The news in the papers might be depressing, the writer added, but he would still have the pleasure of the woodland path and the trees and the mountain air. When we go into nature we are given another chance to taste it, and we should take that opportunity every time it comes our way. Emerson believed in the oneness of creation and recommended the simple life, lived in harmony with nature and with others. I liked poetry at school, particularly the nature poetry of Clare, Masefield and Hardy. In one of Masefield's poems there is the image of 'the shy-eyed delicate deer' trooping down to the pools to drink. It is a beautiful image and one that reminds me vividly of the time I saw four or five red deer gathered together at a mountain stream. It was winter then, the bracken withered and brown on the hills, the heather grey and ragged. It was easy to see how much the deer relished the taste of the clear cold water, filtered as it was over ancient rocks and stones. We are all too apt in this day and age to take water for granted. It is only when something goes wrong, when pipes freeze or burst, that we begin to appreciate again something of its preciousness. This was why it was so lovely to watch the deer at their drinking, the winter sun gilding the rusted fronds of the bracken and making glitters here and there in the stream. Horace wrote that in his prayers he sought a piece of land not so great, a garden with a stream of water ever flowing and a bit of woodland for good measure. In the wintertime, the hare makes do with the withered sedge, but come the spring he looks forward to the sweet taste of grasses and heathers again. It is then that the fields and the bogs open out before him like patchworks of sweetness and promise once more. The rabbits also relish the taste of the grasses, grazing in the long spring evenings.

Meanwhile the stripy badger tugs at earthworms and makes them his delicacy. I have seen a badger feasting on worms more than once, the shimmer of grasses wet with dew all around him in the lateness of evening. Badgers are the most beautiful, most gentle of creatures, their fondness for worms very much part of their charm, though they are also quite partial to fallen fruit in the autumn time. Meanwhile the otter makes a meal of fishes at the water's edge. The wonderfully elongated whiskered otter must surely rank as one of the secret joys of the Irish countryside, his menu made up of eels, minnow, bream and the like. It is wonderful to see an otter swim in the water, his body so superbly streamlined that it has a fluency, a magic all of its own. Nor is there any denying his diving skills, for a single dive may last up to several minutes at a time. Though solitary for much of the year, I have seen them rolling and curling and playing in dark waters at evening time. The red deer loves the taste of heathers and grasses and the young shoots of trees and leaves. Then the birds are at their songs once more, joyfully filling up the copse and the hedge. Already the blackbird is looking forward to the taste of the wild summer fruits, among them the cherries that flourish in the hedge in the month of July. The essayist Joseph Addison had the right idea when it came to blackbirds and cherries: 'I value my garden more for being full of blackbirds than of cherries, and very frankly give them fruit for their songs.' It seemed to have been a fair exchange, and if anything Addison himself got the better of the bargain. It is a wonderful thing to see a blackbird feasting on wild cherries in the hedge, their redness the perfect foil for the blackness of his plumage. It is easy to see how much he relishes the taste, the fruit sometimes poised in his bill for a moment or two, as if the anticipation of the taste is almost as good as the taste itself. A little copse of cherry trees grows by the river and here on long sunny days, when the sun dazzles and shines in the water, the blackbird makes the most of the season's bounty. He savours the taste time and time again and there is a contentment about him.

I remember an old country garden: the robins, the thrushes, the blackbirds coming in search of the soft summer fruits, raspberries, strawberries, blackcurrants. There was a feeling of things being left to run rampant and wild in the garden, of being untrimmed, unchecked, left to their own devices. The fruits were no exception, showing a kind of luxuriance that harked back to their wild state. The little songbirds revelled in the taste and it was as though they were storing up songs for the seasons to come. Whenever anyone walked among the raspberry bushes and canes, or when they made their way to the strawberry beds, there was sure to be a great fluttering of wings as the birds momentarily gave up their feast, but it would not be long until they returned for more. The honeybees come to the nectar wells in search of sweetness and of summer. It is lovely to think of them drinking at these ancient wells that have sustained themselves and their kind for generations. The bees dance their nectar dance all summer long; when they leave the flowers and return to the hive, they perform this dance as their way of indicating the distance and direction of good nectar sources to others. Nectar was said to be the drink of the gods, so it is no great wonder that bees are widely kept in hives for honey. I remember the old man who was proud of his bees. 'Their honey is the honey of flowers and heather,' he said. 'It is the honey of the hills of the sun.' So delicious and beautiful is the taste of honey in summer.

Come the autumn the hedges are full of new delights: plums and damsons, blackberries, apples and haws. The songbirds love the soft wild taste of the blackberries, made rich and plump and juicy by sun and rain. Walt Whitman wrote that a blade of grass was no less than the journey work of the stars, while 'the running blackberry would adorn the parlours of heaven'. Picking blackberries was a favourite pastime when I was young. There was not only the delicious sweetness of the berries, there were the wonders of the hedges, jewelled with butterflies such as the red admiral and the peacock. Though we hardly knew it then, it was a way of being close to nature, the taste of the berries on our lips as we looked for and found the fox's secret trail by the hedge or watched the rabbits at their grazing in the slanted sun of evening. It was a kind of communion with nature, the sun gilding the leaves of the bramble that were already the colour of flame. The blackbirds gathered in the orchard to make a feast of fallen apples. Blackbirds do not generally form flocks, but the temptation of the apples is too great and they may be seen foraging to their hearts' content in the long grasses.

The greenfinches come to the garden for the rosehips they love so much, the greens and yellows of these birds set among the red of the hips. When disturbed, they rise up with a musical twitter, but soon return to their feasting. There are other berries in the garden, those of the well-loved cotoneaster a particular favourite, the branches swaying and shaking when the little birds flit and flutter about them. The siskins are glad of the alder cones, prising the seeds from the cones with little trouble. The goldfinches love the thistle seeds, the gold flashes of their wings giving them a charm all of their own. They are glad of the fruitfulness, the bounty of autumn. The handsome waxwing comes for the berries, among them the berries of the cotoneaster even when it grows against the wall of the house. The waxwing is a rare visitor, coming to these shores only when the berry crop fails in its own territories. Its plumage is a wonderful pinkish buff with a pronounced crest that is swept back on the head. Apart from the predominant pink, there are intricate yellow, white and red markings on the wings and a yellow band at the tip of the dark tail. It is one of the treats of the season to see a waxwing among the berries in the garden. These beautiful birds would surely appreciate the sense of the old Irish saying: 'When the fruit is scarcest its taste is sweetest.'

I remember the icicles hanging from the eaves of the shed. They glimmered and glistened in the cold sun, and when I broke the tip of one of them and put it in my mouth, it tasted like the cold of winter itself.

Nature's gifts are too precious to waste. Earth has a generous nature, though we do not always show our appreciation of it. Its rewards range from the taste of the clear cold mountain water in winter to the delicious sweetness of the fallen apples in autumn. The world is full of such wonder and beauty, it would be foolish not to taste it now and then.

Smelling

A human life, so often likened to a spectacle upon a stage,
is more justly a ritual. The ancient values of dignity, beauty
and poetry which sustain it are of Nature's inspiration; they
are born of the mystery and beauty of the world.

HENRY BESTON

Every star has its place in the sky. Nature celebrates both individuality and community; every star matters among the myriads above. I remember an old country house, the heavy measured beat of the clock, a children's storybook years old. Two children were imagining the nature of the stars. One imagined them as candles held by angels in the windows of the sky. The other thought of them as flowers growing in the gardens of heaven. I liked both ideas even then, but if the stars were flowers, what kind of scent would they have? Perhaps they would have the scent of the midnight blue of the skies when the heavens embrace the dark, for it is the beauty of the dark that enhances the beauty of the stars. In a wood on a cold winter's day, the scent of the trees, the firs, the spruce and the pine, is wonderfully green and winterish. It is the very essence of the season, the verdant freshness filling every part. Maybe it is the crispness, the coldness of the air that enriches the scent, makes it more potent. Smell is probably the most vital sense that animals possess, among them the fox. It is one of the ways in which the dog fox marks the boundaries of his territory. His scent is particularly strong in the wintertime when it seems to hang suspended in the frozen air, his *wo-wo* barking carrying far and wide across the woods and fields.

In the winter garden, the gaultheria is hung with bright red berries, emerging from the small white bellflowers of July. The leaves are wonderfully aromatic, and when crushed release the strongest scent of wintergreen. In the past, the leaves of gaultheria were used to produce oil of wintergreen by distillation, this oil was then used to make ointments for the relief of muscular pain. The seed heads of the sumac look resplendent in the sun, their burgundy reds catching the light from the east. Sumac has become widely popular in many gardens but the seeds can be ground down to make a sweet spice, used in Greek and Middle Eastern cookery.

Spring brings the sweet scent of grasses, which the hares and the rabbits seem to love. The smell of rosemary gladdens the herb garden, the aroma of the grey-green evergreen leaves still widely used in cookery and in the manufacture of perfumes. It will not be long until the scent of the old-fashioned lilacs will be gladdening the hedges again.

The scent of newly mown grasses at the start of summer is truly beautiful. The long swathes of hay are left to dry in the summer sun, the confetti colour of all the wild flowers crisping up. The scent of the honeysuckle, the woodbine, is delicious in the hedge, all the more potent on long summer evenings. There are garden varieties of the honeysuckle but the wild species is more than a match for any of them. The ornithologist W. H. Hudson wrote in the year 1903:

> After sunset the fragrance of the honeysuckle is almost too much: standing near the blossom-laden hedge, when there is no wind to dissipate the odour, there is a heaviness in it which makes it like some delicious honeyed liquor which we are drinking in.

The scent of the gorse is also like honey, especially in the bogs where great brakes of it run yellow and golden under the sun. It is the singing stall of the linnet and the stonechat, the scent and the song deliciously jumbled together in the warmth of the summer's day. I have put a few of the scented flowers in my pocket more than once as a memento, a keepsake of the summer. The meadow would not be the meadow without the scent of the clovers red and white. Red clover is known in Irish as *seamair dhearg*, sometimes also called *seamair chapaill*, literally horse clover. The scent is delicious on lazy summer afternoons when it seems to become the signature of the hour. The American novelist Henry James wrote that the two most beautiful words in the English language were 'Summer afternoon – summer afternoon'. The red clover is an important source of nectar for hive bees, and clover honey is regarded as one of the best of all.

The scent of the white clover is equally delicious. I remember an old summer meadow, the black Kerry cows grazing in the lush wild swards of white clover above the infinite blue of the bay. The cows were sleek, diminutive and graceful, looking like creatures from myth and legend, the great expanse of clover spreading far and wide at their feet. Behind them the old ringed fairy fort provided the perfect backdrop for a painter's canvas.

The blooms of the dog rose may not have the fragrance of their more cosseted garden counterparts, but they have their moments. The downy biennial evening primrose is not a native plant, but rather an introduction from North America. It is now well-established in some of its favourite habitats, including roadsides and railway tracks, sunny banks, sand dunes and waste places. The large yellow, glossy flowers open at night and are attractive to moths because of their subtle fragrance. It is said that every flower lasts one night only.

Evening primrose also has a sweet-tasting root which is sometimes eaten in salads, but it is the subtlety of the fragrance that gives it its special charm. The delicious scent has been compared to that of orange blossom. The fantastic meadowsweet loves the damp meadows and marshes, as well as the borders of streams and ponds. It produces frothy heads of creamy, sweetly-scented white flowers. The scent has a kind of languor about it on sultry afternoons, so much so that it was sometimes thought to induce drowsiness. It is another of those striking, old-fashioned plants and it gives good value as it flowers from June to September. I remember an old country kitchen, a blue and white jug on the window brimming with sprays of meadowsweet and vibrant, purple loosestrife, the perfect foil for the creamy froth of the strongly scented meadowsweet.

The water mint flourishes in wet ground, damp meadows, and on the edges of ponds and ditches. The individual flowers are tiny: lilac pink in colour with four petals. The plant has long been used in herb medicine in the preparation of peppermint tea, but more than that it is a great favourite with a variety of insects. Corn mint grows in arable fields and meadows, its small lilac flowers borne in dense whorls, spaced at intervals along the stem. Daisy-like feverfew is found in waste ground, roadside verges and stony places. The yellow discs and white ray florets are part of the magic of summer in the country. Densely branched and aromatic, it was, as the name implies, once used in the treatment of fevers. Yarrow and tansy boast their own aromas, the flowers of the former borne in flat clusters of pinkish white, those of the latter yellow in flat-topped clusters. There is something wonderfully antique and ancient about these gorgeous plants; they and their kind have been scenting summer for as long as memory and beyond. The pineapple mayweed blooms from May to November. It may not be the most inspiring of plants to look at, but the leaves smell wonderfully of pineapple when crushed. Once a native of North America and East Asia, it now grows wild on waste ground of all kinds. As it seems to be able to withstand any amount of trampling, it is also found growing on paths, still flowering although almost trodden to the ground.

The fragrant orchid, as its name suggests, is known and loved for its scent. The pink violet flowers are borne on tall spikes, the leaves on the stem long, narrow and lance-shaped. This is another of the jewels of summer, flowering from May to August, and finding a home in damp grasslands, especially those rich in lime. There are many other varieties of wild orchid growing in Ireland, among them the common spotted orchid and the bee orchid, but neither has the scent of their fragrant counterpart. It is lamentable that it has become rarer in many parts, especially in the east.

The butterflies love the scent of the buddleia, the butterfly bush. They crowd its showy spikes of honey-scented flowers, lilac or white, their silken flutterings epitomising the majesty of summer. All of the large daisy-like flowers are enjoyed by butterflies for their plentiful supply of nectar and for their firm support. These include single dahlias and chrysanthemums and especially michaelmas daisies, which flower in late September and October. It is wonderful to see a host of butterflies crowding the blooms of the buddleia on long summer days.

The fragrance of the flowers, grasses under the hedge, the margins smelling of ripened damsons, plums and blackberries: it is as though the world is overflowing with the goodness of autumn's store, the scent of the fruits a feast in itself, particularly potent when the evenings are dewy and damp and the mist hangs low on the hills. In the orchard the air is filled with the cidery scent of fallen apples, and not only the foxes but the badgers come to make the most of them, the soft autumnal moon lying on its back overhead.

Nature's ways may sometimes appear cruel to us. Though driven as they are by the instinct for survival, they may not, in nature's terms, be cruel at all. William Blake wrote that 'cruelty has a human heart', reminding us that we are hardly in a position to judge. It must be acknowledged that nature is sometimes 'red in tooth and claw', as Tennyson has it, though this does not deny us the right to celebrate the beauty that is all around us. It should, if anything, make its preciousness more apparent, inviting us to to cherish it all the more.

Epilogue

Beauty, they say, lies in the eye of the beholder. If that is the case, then it lies in the hearing, tasting, touching and smelling of the beholder too. The Scottish philosopher David Hume said: 'Beauty is no quality in things themselves; it exists merely in the mind which contemplates them.' He might equally have written the sense which perceives them, for sensory perception comes first, then the feeling, the emotion, and finally the intellectual response. Wordsworth wrote of the pleasures of meditation 'slipping in between the beauty coming and the beauty gone'. It is a charming image suggesting remembrance of things past and anticipation of things to come. He was a great believer in the power of beauty to live on in the memory, even long after it has been seen and felt in the heart. He expressed this very simply in his poem 'Daffodils', where he remembered all the joy and delight the flowers had given him when he and his sister Dorothy had gone for a country stroll:

> For oft when on my couch I lie
> In vacant or in pensive mood,
> They flash upon the inward eye
> Which is the bliss of solitude;
> And then my heart with pleasure fills,
> And dances with the daffodils.

He returned to the same theme in 'Tintern Abbey'. The 'beauteous forms' which he had seen in nature came back to him in lonely rooms, bringing with them 'sensations sweet', amid the noise and din of the city. He felt the good of them in the blood and the heart before they passed into the 'purer mind' with the promise of peace and restoration. For Wordsworth then, beauty and memory were clearly allied, for the remembrance of beautiful things meant peace and serenity. No wonder that he talked of an eye made quiet by the power of harmony and the deep power of joy. It was with such an eye that he could see into the life of all things. For the Russian poet and novelist Boris Pasternak, beauty was the joy of possessing form and form was the key to organic life and nature, since no living thing could survive without it. Poet Edmund Spenser said the same centuries earlier:

> That beauty is not, as fond men misdeem,
> An outward show of things that only seem...
> For of the soul the body form doth take:
> For soul is form and doth the body make.

The poet James Elroy Flecker wrote of poets 'who swear that beauty lives though lilies die'. One of my favourite poets at school was Walter de la Mare and a poem that I liked in particular was 'Farewell'. Its message was very simple – we should not go to bed at night without counting our blessings, remembering and giving thanks for the beauty that is all around us. All of the beautiful things that we love were taken from those who loved them in other days. John Keats wrote in one of his letters:

> 'If I should die,' said I to myself, 'I have left no immortal work behind me – nothing to make my friends proud of my memory – but I have loved the principle of beauty in all things, and if I had had time I would have made myself remembered.'

He saw beauty as the ultimate truth:

> I am certain of nothing but the holiness of the heart's affections and the truth of imagination; what the imagination seizes as beauty must be truth, whether it existed before or not.

G. H. Lewes, the common-law husband of George Eliot, had ideas of his own on the nature of beauty:

Many a genius has been slow of growth. Oaks that flourish for a thousand years do not spring up into beauty like a reed.

I love the contrast between the oak and the reed, between the slow beauty of the one and the sudden, almost instantaneous beauty of the other. However, it is the very transience of beauty that impels us to celebrate it and to keep it in memory thereafter. The bond between beauty and memory is inseparable, for if beauty brings peace, then so too does the memory of it. How many times have I myself used the phrase 'I remember' in these pages? I remember the delight of walking in an old wood in springtime, the first of the crocuses, purple and golden springing to life everywhere around, the rooks, homely and familiar, flapping and fluttering among the bare boughs overhead, and thinking of new beginnings. I remember the cuckoo calling from the cover of the beech trees in the old school grove, soft and muffled like the voice of summer itself, the light pouring through the wild and vivid greens. I remember the handsome pine marten climbing a pine tree in autumn, the rich chocolate-brown of his fur, the cream patch at his throat barely visible. I remember the little field mouse in the yard in the snow, making quick sorties here and there before retreating to the safety of his nest in the nearby old stone wall. One of Thomas Hood's most famous poems is simply called, 'I Remember, I Remember':

I remember, I remember,
The roses red and white,
The violets and the lily cups,
Those flowers made of light!

The lilacs where the robins built,
And where my brother set
The laburnum on his birthday,
The tree is living yet!

When we remember the beauty of nature we come again 'into the peace of wild things', for they are not burdened with the baggage of the past nor anxious at the thought of the future. Rather they live in the moment and make the most of it. A love of beauty and the remembrance of it can be our pathway to peace. As the old medieval proposition goes, 'God and nature do nothing in vain.'

When I read Sylvia Plath's poem, 'Black Rook in Rainy Weather', I wasn't sure if I liked it, or even understood it at first. I grew to like it over time however. It is a very modern poem in the way that it expresses not only the poet's fatigue and disconnection with the world around her, but also her longing to belong: to be loved and be part of the natural world. Though she wavers between doubt and conviction, she knows that moments of beauty, even the smallest of moments, can make a difference to her life. They have done so in the past and they may do so again. This is why the sight of the rook rearranging its feathers in the rain can 'shine' for her and lift her spirit once more. It can lead her out of that which she fears most: emptiness and 'neutrality'.

The beauty that we see around us is the visible, tangible expression of the pulse, the heartbeat, the life-force that lies at the very heart of the universe. It is in our own interest to cherish and protect it. We tamper with it at our peril, for being part of it we suffer the consequences that flow from our neglect. As the Native American Chief Seattle put it: 'Man did not weave the web of life. He is merely a strand in it. Whatever he does to the web, he does to himself.' There are times when we get our sense of belonging back to front. The earth does not belong to us: we belong to it. It is easy to be dismissive of the gift of the senses, yet it is a wonderful gift which allows us to perceive and appreciate the beauty of the world around us. It allows us to embrace the world of colours and sounds, tastes, textures and scents – an uplifting and enriching experience. There is a tendency however to regard the senses as being somewhat inferior to the emotions, the spirit and the intellect. Yet the senses are our gateway, our portal to engage with the beauty of the world. They give us a perception without which we could not appreciate or understand it. The senses are the foundation on which so much else rests. If we believe that creation is an expression of the Word of God, if it is in fact a revelation of that Word, then it is written in the language of colours, sounds, tastes, textures and scents. It is an expression of the divine written in a way to which human senses can relate. Just as one sense seldom comes into play on its own, but rather acts in unison with the rest, so too are the senses connected to the emotions, the spirit and the intellect. The senses may be seen as the nurturers of our spiritual, emotional and intellectual being. They are the channels that can lead us to love, hope and understanding. They help us to appreciate that the beauty of the universe, for all its richness and diversity, still has the imprint of unity. It is a unity embracing diversity, the colours of the flowers of the field like echoes of the far-flung stars, the music of the rain like the music of the senses touching the heart and the soul. Only then do we begin to see that the earth and the heavens are bounded by the one great circumference: the circumference of beauty.

Nature's beauty is not just the beauty of form. It is the beauty of rhythm and movement and energy; birds in flight above shining water, the sweep of the fox through a sunlit grove, the changeful embrace of light and shadow, the surge of the ocean wave, the long parallels gleaming and shining far and away to the edge of the horizon. The cycles of nature, the circles of the seasons bring us the reassurance that the earth never grows tired or weary or disheartened, but maintains a continuous flow. Sometimes I think that those who walk in nature never walk alone for they have the trees and the birds and the flowers for company. They have the meadows and the seas and the stars, the joy of the lonely shore. When I walk in the wavy green meadows, foaming with flowers at the height of summer, I cannot resist the impulse to recline in the warm grasses. There is a delicious sense of wonder and delight in lying there among the flowers and the grasses, looking up at the marvellous blue of the sky. Sometimes it puts me in mind of the blue of the eggs of the hedge sparrow, the purest of blues, or of the song thrush, or even the chaffinch. It makes me think of my childhood, when I was a boy and I lay on the warm grasses, my sheepdog Rover a constant companion by my side. He preferred it, of course, when I went running helter-skelter with him in the long grasses, the silken swish of the grasses soft against my skin and his coat. Looking back, as I lay there on the grass, it was as if I was at one with the earth, if only for a short while. It was almost as if I were part of the all-embracing beauty of grasses and flowers and sky, as if summer were making me one of its own. I would run through the fields to the edge of the ocean, the soft waves breaking and falling at my feet, the mountains blue and hazy waved against the rim of the sky, the old sandstone cliffs standing like sentinels. When a butterfly went flitting past, or came to rest on a flower, it was just another reminder of how beautiful summer could be. It was the same when the marvellous blue-black swallows came skimming down the blue hills of sky, or the frog sat still in the margins in the shade of the wild woodbine. Sometimes as we grow older we can lose our sense of wonder and delight in the beauty of the world around us. It is still part of our birthright, however, part of our humanity, and nature still invites us to reclaim it and make it our own once more.

*I once had a sparrow alight upon my shoulder for a moment
while I was hoeing in a village garden, and I felt that I was
more distinguished by that circumstance than I should have
been by any epaulette I could have worn.*

HENRY DAVID THOREAU